"If you find it hard to laugh at yourself, I would be happy to do it for you"

Groucho Marx

After years of working in Advertising, and after spending days and weeks talking and discussing about very urgent and super important stuff with colleagues, clients and partners, I decided to start gathering all those silly and non-sense things we all end up saying or hearing while working in this industry.

So sit back, relax and have a bit of a laugh about the unfamous agency life. Enjoy!

"Can you please send me the logo in 'pectoral'?"
(Client, Advertising Head, meaning 'vectorial' for vector graphics)

"Before negotiating something, I practice in the shower"
(Client, Marketing Assistant)

"They loved it but they want to change the pictures, the headline and the design"
(Agency, Account Executive sharing feedback)

"Could you please make the thought bubbles in this ad more realistic?"
(Client to Designer)

> "Quit asking smart questions and just do what the client says"

(Agency, Account Executive to Copywriter)

> "I have a degree in Art History, so i know all about this advertising stuff"

(Client, to Copywriter)

> "Let's keep this in 'stand bike'"

(Media, Writer, meaning 'stand-by')

"I'm going home, we're presenting the campaign tomorrow. Have you started with the pieces yet? Let me take a quick look, I just want to see the logos"

(Agency, Account Executive)

"What's going on? I do a search in the Family category images and I got a picture of two guys and a kid!"
(Agency, Head of Production)

"What does the Red Cross logo look like?"
(Client to designer for health services logo)

"There is no creative brief because I didn't feel like writing one"
(Agency, Account Executive to Copywriter)

"I am well aware that I continually screw you over"
(Agency, President to Copywriter)

"If there's a brief, it's a mistake"
(Agency, Account Executive)

"That's very beautiful. I mean it's huge! Exactly what we need. But we're not ready for it. We're gonna have too many contact and clients with that website. It's a problem for us. Can we have a break and finish when we'll be a bigger business?"
(Client, about a corporate website)

"We are a small company. If we were a big company we would worry about what is best for the brand. Since we are small, we need to worry about the budget"
(Client, Marketing Manager)

"I like it, but I just don't think a multinational company should be doing ads in felt tip"

(Client, on first presentation of a line drawing concept scamp)

"10am meeting! I don't even get up before 10am…"

(Agency, Creative to Account Executive)

"This sky is too much of a dusk and too little of a dawn. Are we sure this is the dawn we saw yesterday?"
(Client, Brand Manager who was present on a shooting at 4 o'clock in the morning)

"So the TV ad is going to be a cartoon?"
(Client, when reviewing storyboards)

"I always wear a blazer to shoots cause then everyone knows I'm the client"
(Client, VP Marketing at TV shoot)

"I can't start until I see the creative brief. You gave me the brief?" - *"Oh, I must have thrown it away"*
(Agency, Creative to Account Executive)

"I'd like to use a photo of ground zero for an ad. One where we can see a pipe like our client's product in the background" - "Oh, is the client making a contribution to a victim's fund or something?" - "No, I don't think so." - "So, what, you just want to capitalize on the situation?" - "I wouldn't call it that"
(Agency, Account Executive to creative team during briefing)

"Do you need the images in 'high residue' or 'low residue'? You probably need the low-res, right?"

(Client, preparing to send a bunch of images to Account Executive)

"Make it wild but conservative!"

(Agency, Account Executive, to Art Director)

"I'm the one who sets the priorities around here, and my stuff is always at the top of the list"
(Agency Owner to Designer)

"When do you need the prints for?" - "We need this printed ASAP, but it's not like we need it tomorrow or anything"
(Client, answering to graphic designer)

"I just sent you a link to something you've got to read." - "The link isn't working. I can't click it." - "Then just copy and paste it in your browser." - "I don't know what you're talking about. I've never copied and pasted anything. Can you come down here and show me?"

(Agency, conversation between Creative and Senior Account Strategist)

"Dude, you just booked my pitch team which is due tomorrow for ANOTHER pitch?" - "Hey, I don't do f…ing operations"
(Agency, conversation between Senior Creative Director and CEO/COO)

"How many weeks are in a 13 week cycle?"
(Account Executive to Producer)

"I probably should have told you this in the beginning... I have a personal vendetta against standard serif typefaces. Can we redo the whole thing in Gill Sans?"

(Client, Administrative Director to Designer, hours before print run)

"You have to have the layout tomorrow" - "I never got the brief!" - "I told you about it on my way to the men's room"
(Agency, Account Executive to Creative)

"I like... takes 1 and 3!"
(Client, on hearing the same V/O played 4 times)

"An ad doesn't have to be memorable to be good"

(Agency, Associate Creative Director to a client in an effort to submarine a junior team's work competing with his own)

"This is a picture of how I want the ad. I had to draw it in a napkin"

(Client, Marketing Manager)

"Well, it's OK. It's just that we just want mediocre advertising. We don't really want to stand out"

(Client, to Agency Team concerning new branding campaign presented)

"Can you make the hamster look less ambitious? Can we minute that?"

(Client to Agency)

"When do you need the prints for?" - *"We need this printed ASAP, but it's not like we need it tomorrow or anything"*
(Client, answering to graphic designer)

"52k? Isn't that a bit expensive for one banner?"
(Client)

"The client loves your ad, she really does. She wanted me to tell you that. She just wants to change the visual and the headline"

(Agency, Account Executive to creative team)

"Not cliché enough. We need a recast!"

(Client, in pre production meeting for a commercial)

"Really… real-LY… REAL-ly… I'm not sure this word is doing it for me. Come up with a better word than 'really'"
(Agency, Senior Writer to Junior Writer)

"One of the images you used shows too much teeth… and people are put off by too much teeth"
(Agency, Account Executive to Designer)

"The voiceovers for the videos in German, English, French, Spanish and Italian are good, but the voices are all different! Can't we have them all done by the same guy?"
- "And who do you want to do them? The Pope?"
(Client, giving feedback to Account Executive)

"We don't need a full re-design of our website, we just want to change the look and feel to be more professional. You know new colors, photos, and change some of the graphical elements"

(Client to Designer)

"Well, it's OK. It's just that we just want mediocre advertising. We don't really want to stand out"
(Client, to Agency Team concerning new branding campaign presented)

"Adapt concept to billboard, 40 feet by 60 feet. For presentation, please make actual-sized mock-up"
(Agency, Account Manager to Art Director)

"My wife just remodeled our family room in burgundy and gray, I really liked that. Let's use those colors for the annual report"
(Client, Executive Director, to Designer)

"If I give you approval, what can I still change?"
(Client, Marketing Manager)

"How can I put the link on my desktop when you know I only have a laptop?"
(IT Client to Agency)

"How do you print screen?" - "Alt-Print Screen" - "So, how long does it take to print?"
(Agency, Account Manager)

"I will contact the artist, what is his name?" - "Vincent Van Gogh" - "Ok, I will call him and get his approval"

(Agency, Account Executive to Art Director on being told that ´Sunflowers´ cannot be used in the layout)

"Can we lose the clouds? Clouds are not professional"

(Client, CEO giving feedback)

"What copy should I use?" - "Just do some of that fluff that you do"
(Agency, Creative Director)

"Let me be frank" - "Fine. Be Frank or be Jeff but pick one face and stick with it"
(Agency, Account Executive turning on creative after earlier praising the work)

"When can I see the draft of the event report for the newsletter?" - *"End of next Monday?"* - *"No. I want it today. I need to show it to my boss to get his approval"* - *"Er... but the event is this Friday. So I can't interview guests for their comments and do a report of the event until the event happens right?"* - *"I don't care. I want the draft by the end of today. This the way we always work. Other agencies have done this for us before. So why can't you?"*

(Conversation between Client and Copywriter)

"We haven't even done a brochure for America and you're doing one for another country!"

(Client to the creative team after seeing a brochure with Loren Ipsum copy)

"Should we really be spending 2 million dollars on this if the World is going to end?"

(Client to Agency about launching a website right before the year 2000)

"We're heading to the Grand Canyon. Has anyone ever gone down (Grand Canyon) in a helicopter?" - "No, but I've gone down on a donkey"

(Client and Agency, conference call discussing planning)

"Here's a picture of the front door of my house. I designed it myself, back in the seventies. Could you incorporate the design in our new site?"
(Client briefing the Designer)

"I like it, but it's too single-minded"
(Client to Art Director after concept presentation)

"There is too much of the mother's nipple visible. I think breast feeding mothers will be offended by this"
(Client feedback to Art Director)

"We need something that has never been done before. Find out how everybody else did it - and do that"
(Client, Brand Manager who wanted a promotion)

"Can you add a drop shadow or bevel to the logo?"
(Client to Designer)

"I'm sending you a 100 kilowatts photograph. Is it good for printing?"
(Client, IT Manager)

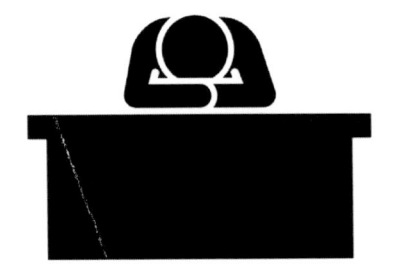

"Can you redesign the business cards in Microsoft Word so we can change the names ourselves?"
(Client to Designer)

"I think translating this piece to another language is a great idea in the future, but can you translate the Greek to English when we print it?"
(Client, Brand Manager, in response to the Lorem Ipsum)

"Concept 1 is approved. Although why don't you show me something that incorporates concept 1 with concept 3 and uses the headline from concept 2? Make the logo bigger like in concept 2 and the copy larger from concept 3. You guys did a great job, you are right on target with concept 1"
(Client, Brand Manager)

"I can't help you now. I have to go to a teamwork seminar"

(Agency, Account Executive to Creative Team in a moment of client-related crisis)

"Can we add sound effects? People love sound effects!"

(Client to creative team, after being presented a radio campaign)

"In a perfect world, if there was no Christmas, when could we launch?"

(Client to Creative Director complaining about the production schedule because time set aside for the holidays and agency /office closures conflicted with their desired in-market date)

"Can you adjust the leading on the headline?" - *"No, the font comes like that"*

(Agency, Art Director's reply to Account Manager)

"Hey, is 44 kb good?" - "No it's really small" - "I don't understand, it's large on my screen and when I open it up it says 300 pixels"
(Agency, Creative Director, confusing pixels with DPI)

"You don't have to do it tonight. I want it on my desk at 9 am"
(Creative Director, leaving the agency at 6 pm, to Art Director)

"Tell him it doesn't snow at any of the Hawaii properties, but maybe we can do the same effect with molten lava spew"

(Agency, Designer to Project Manager, after the client forwards a link to a snow animation on a holiday website)

"We need you to resize the Portuguese and Spanish versions" - "I don't think I ever did a Spanish version. I mean, I remember doing one in Mexican…"

(Agency, Art Director talking to a Retoucher)

"I hate to tell you but that idea's been done before" - "I know, but it was in England. Nobody's done it here so it's not stealing"
(Agency, Anonymous)

"Is that Spanish?"
(Client, watching a draft with Lorem Ipsum placeholder text)

"Could you move our logo to the top of the poster? I mean, what if someone is standing in front of it?"

(Client to Creative Director)

"I don't like green. Can we change it?"

(Client, Account Director to Art Director, personally unhappy with the colour of giant multinational coffee chain logo)

"I need awards! get me awards! If you don't get me awards, otherwise I will make sure you get fired before I do"
(Client, Marketing Manager to Agency Account Director)

"Can you make the cursive font more cursive?"
(Client to Art Director)

"Here's a picture of the front door of my house. I designed it myself, back in the seventies. Could you incorporate the design in our new site?
(Client briefing the Designer)

"That cover is too hip for the room"
(Client, giving feedback about a brochure cover for a church)

"This logo isn't the right size" - "Well, I have the file open in Photoshop and the dimensions are correct" - "That can't be right. I'm measuring it and it's about an 1/8" too small" - "How are you measuring it?" - "I'm holding my ruler up to the monitor"

(Client and Agency, phone conversation reviewing a JPEG)

"Why don't we cast a 50-year old that looks like 38?"

(Client and Art Director disagree on how old the model should be... Account Executive comes up with brilliant compromise)

"OK, so what background color do you want?" - "I don't know. You guys are the professionals"

(Conversation between Creative and Client)

"I know you guys don't like to steal creative work, but sometimes the best ideas come from other places"
(Agency, Associate Creative Director, trying to get his Creative team to copy a banner)

"I know that you are out today but if you have a sec to look at these to give me some feedback that would be great…"
(Agency, Producer to Art Director)

"The ad looks great, but I can't hear it" - "Have you tried adjusting the volume?" - "Oh, that's much better"

(Client, on a phone call giving feedback to Editor)

"We want it to sound like a brick hitting a parachute"

(Client to Audio Producer)

"Don't worry about the talent's wardrobe sizes. I don't want to bother them anymore. Besides, there are lot's of places to buy clothes near the shoot"

(Agency, Account Executive to Art Director)

"Should we really be spending 2 million dollars on this if the World is going to end?"
(Client to Agency about launching a website right before the year 2000)

"Today's time management seminar has been cancelled due to a scheduling conflict"
(Agency President)

"Can we remove the french things on the word 'résumé'?"
(Client, Marketing Manager to Designer)

"Why do we need to code the website? Can't you just export from Microsoft Word?"
(Agency, Chairman of an Internet Company)

"There's a lot of empty space in this ad, but I'm just not sure that the audience we are targeting is the empty-space audience"

(Agency, Account manager to Designer)

"Does white count as a color?"

(Client referring to white paper while looking at a brochure)

> "How can you solve a major mess in 3 days? With promises, not with facts"
> (Agency, Account Director)

> "When will the 'brochette' be ready?"
> (Agency, Owner, meaning 'brochure')

"I need to speak to the Chairman" - "You can't, he's out on an unbreakable out of agency commitment" - "Huh?" - "OK, don't tell anyone, he's playing golf with his brother"

(Agency, conversation between Creative and Chairman´s PA)

"So that's the concept and the site name. What are your thoughts?" - *"I'm just trying to imagine a logo with a name that long"* - *"Don't worry about it son, we'll leave that up to the designers"*

(Agency, conversation between CEO and Lead Designer)

"I don't want any of you in here working on Thanksgiving Day"

(Agency, Creative Director, thinking he's being generous)

"Of course you want it for yesterday! If you want it for today, you should order it TOMORROW"

(Agency, Anonymous)

"I like this layout, but let me take it home and show my wife. She's the artist in the family"

(Client to Agency, about wife who was taking a painting class)

"Oh, they must want those secret magic words that mean four things at once"

(Agency, Copywriter to Account Manager, discussing client comments)

"Could you possibly give us a design for the business card that's more like the one our CEO designed in PowerPoint?"
(Client, Marketing Director to Designer)

"Could you move our logo to the top of the poster? I mean… What if someone is standing in front of it?"
(Client to Creative Director)

"I know the globe is in our logo but we are not a global company so the only globe should be the one in our logo"
(Client feedback)

"Logo needs to be bigger on the front page, so it can be seen across a room if in a brochure stand"
(Client, to Designer)

"We love option 1. It's the cleanest one. We'd just like to add some information. Just the Call to Action, website and our partner's logos. You are the artists. Do your thing so it doesn't look like too much info. Gosh, I love it! It's so clean!"

(Client, Advertising Coordinator to Agency Account Supervisor, making comments on a what was intending to be a clean Billboard art)

"There's a lot of empty space in this ad, but I'm just not sure that the audience we are targeting is the empty-space audience"
(Agency, Account manager to Designer)

"My sky is not as blue as my competitors' sky!"
(Client, viewing his spot)

"We don't know what we don't know. We just don't know"
(Agency, Executive Creative Director)

"Don't worry, this project is really just a graphic design exercise, it doesn't require any real thinking or anything"
(Agency, Account Executive to Designer)

"Don't be so clever. Not everyone gets double endondas"

(Agency Owner to Copywriter, meaning… 'innuendos')

"Well Susan, after all this time you know how we work" - *"Jim, my name is Stacy"*

(Agency, Creative Director to long time client)

"Please call me in an hour… but I will not answer because I am in a meeting"
(Agency, Client Service Director to Client)

"It's already a pizza, now with what the client is asking for, it'll make it an all-dressed pizza"
(Agency, Project Manager to his Director of Production)

"It´s all ok. good looking, nice layout, modern, right concept, but my appreciation about it is: the black is too dark, and the red is too bloody"
(Client, Product Manager, giving feedback to CD)

"But this campaign is a 'copy page' of the previous one!"
(Client, Marketing Manager)

"What do you mean this is a four color job? I don't want four colors, we are paying for ALL of the colors, and by God I want ALL of the colors"
(Client, Marketing Manager to agency Art Director)

"Man, my head REALLY hurts. This working all day thing is killing me" - "Yeah… but it's only 4:30 pm"
(Agency, conversation between Art Director and Copywriter)

"It's important to state that this event will take place on the first day of Spring. We can incorporate that in the communication, in the layout as well as in the frame of the communication. But we don't want it to be highlighted in the communication"
(Client, extracted from a brief)

"You need to add a a line on the cover of the invitation that says how to open it" - "Huh? But its a tri-fold…. How do they not know how to open it?" - "The client can't figure out how to open it. Just add 'open here, dude'"

(Agency, between Art Director and Associate Creative Director regarding client revision request)

"Let's open up the text box more to alleviate the bad text 'raping'"
(Agency, email from Associate Creative Director to Creative team, attempting to comment on text 'wrapping')

"Please include this disclaimer: The clinical significance of non-clinical data is unknown"
(Pharma client to interactive agency)

"This logo needs to be extremely high end" - *"So like Ralph Lauren black label?"* - *"Higher- but don't spend more than 3 hours on it, it's not that important"*
(Agency, VP to Creative Director regarding a logo for a golf outing)

"The good news is, you have the weekend to work"
(Agency, Traffic to Creative Team)

"It's simple really: I want you to come up with something that's never been done before; something that touches hearts and minds all around the world. Oh, and I need it by 11 tomorrow morning"
(Agency, Marketing Director to Creative team)

"Can you make the URL resemble a web link? You know, underlined in blue. That way everyone knows it's for our web site"
(Client, to Account Manager, describing the URL in a print ad)

"We really like working with you, so lets try not to get lawyers involved"

(Client, President to Freelance Graphic Designer)

"I'm a channel agnostic" - "…a what? Oh, f... off with your stupid terms"

(Agency, Conversation between Media girl and Client)

"I'm good at what I do, but I don't necessarily know what I am doing"
(Client, regarding their position at their company)

"The spot is great except for the graphics and colors" - *"But we duplicated the graphics and colors from your tri-fold, website and menu"* - *"Yes, we don't like those"*
(Client, to Account Executive in reference to TV commercial sent out for approval)

"We want to put a yellow submarine, like The Beatles song, in this ad"
(Client to Copywriter, for an industrial paint ad)

"These measures for the ad, are they live area or trim?" - "As you prefer!"
(Agency, Account Executive)

"Can't you make that dog smile? Don't you have a smile filter on this expensive machine?"
(Agency, Owner)

"The client wants the image moved over a little more" - *"Ok, about how many pixels?"* - *"I don't know what a pixel is. I can only think in inches…"*
(Agency, Project Manager to Graphic Designer regarding a simple change)

"We don't care for the black bar under the photo in our ad. It might make people think of death too much. Can we change it to a green gradient?"
(Client, to Graphic Designer regarding changes to an ad promoting their war memorial. Black bar in question was under a photo of a cemetery)

"Make it edgy… but not too edgy"
(Agency, HR Manager)

"We have to make an effort this quarter"
(Agency, President, sent from his phone while he was on vacation at a beach)

"We need to send the client a JPG of the image as soon as possible" -
"Sure. Do you think the JPG will fit in this size envelope?"
(Agency, Intern to another intern, who was holding up an actual 6x9 envelope)

"We need the beach to come down farther on the page, but this has to be done quickly. Just use the 'sand filter' in Photoshop or something…"

(Agency, Account Executive to production artist)

"We do understand we need to use the required brand standard templates, but at the same time, we thought the layouts would be less template-y"
(Agency, Project Manager)

"I see orange as between, like, yellow and red"
(Agency, Designer explaining his color choice for a logo)

"I can't start until I see the creative brief. You gave me the brief?" - "Oh, I must have thrown it away"
(Agency, Creative to Account Executive)

"This brochure needs to be more literal, at the bottom of each page of the brochure add the words 'Turn Page'"
(Client, Brand Manager)

"We really should go after these guys. They're right in our back door"

(Agency owner at staff meeting, emphasizing the need to go after nearby businesses, ignoring that the phrase was "right in our backyard")

"You don't even need to show me that campaign, because I already know I'm going to hate it"

(Agency, Account Executive to creative team)

"This product has no features that are better than the competition, so there's no US. We expect the agency to find one"
(Client, briefing the Agency)

"Your work is really perfect. But, it's too good for us, therefore we decided for a different agency"
(Client's feedback on a lost pitch)

"I know that you are out today but if you have a sec to look at these to give me some feedback that would be great…"
(Agency, Producer to Art Director)

"Which Pantone color did you use?" - "I don't know, they change those numbers every year"
(Agency, Art Director, asking to a very junior artist)

"I need a banner with a dynamic looking basketball, but it can't look like a basketball. It needs to look like a volleyball too"
(Agency, Account executive to graphic designer)

"Sorry, that brief has fallen off the radar" - "This aint the bloody cold war"
(Agency, Conversation between Account Executive and Client)

"This ad has been approved. Can you adapt it to print on the surface of a pen?"
(Agency, Account Executive)

"When you come to the meeting, could you bring that 'Mastone' thing for colors?"
(Agency, Account Executive, meaning… 'Pantone')

"Well, actually, we have to say this but without saying it"
(Agency, Account Executive, briefing)

"Please rewrite the letter so that it will yield less response, as our call center is understaffed"
(Client brief to Agency)

"You don't have to do it tonight. I want it on my desk at 9 am"

(Creative Director, leaving the agency at 6 pm, to Art Director)

"I know there are a lot of typos, but your budget didn't cover Quality Control"

(Post Production Account rep to client)

"It needs to EXPLODE off the page! It needs FIREWORKS and COLOR! LOTS of colors! And exclamation points! Be creative. I could have done what you sent me on my own computer. The 14pt type is so small. I mean, you guys are the experts..."

(Hospital client, reacting to a double-truck newspaper ad celebrating being chosen ´Reader's Choice´ for hospitals in a conference call to the AE, CD, AD and CW)

"The client wants the image moved over a little more" - "Ok, about how many pixels?" - "I don't know what a pixel is. I can only think in inches..."
(Agency, Project Manager to Graphic Designer regarding a simple change)

"Why do you need a brief? You saw the SOW, didn't you? Just work from that"
(Agency, Account director to a Creative Director on why a creative brief is superfluous)

"I probably won't get to it until tomorrow because today is my birthday and I'm trying to get out of here'"
(Agency, Creative Director to Agency Project Manager when asked to provide final art for microsite to be launched in 2 days)

"Hi, have you got a minute? Oh, I see you're busy. I'll pop by later then…" - "That's alright, I can talk to you without listening"
(Agency, Copywriter comes into agency boss's office)

"Please make the copy less exciting. We want people to come and pay to go to the conference, but we don't want them to think it will be enjoyable once they get here"
(Client, to a Copywriter)

"I probably won't get to it until tomorrow because today is my birthday and I'm trying to get out of here"

(Agency, Creative Director to Agency Project Manager when asked to provide final art for microsite to be launched in 2 days)

"I want the site to look expensive and cheap at the same time"

(Client briefing)

"I think we should redesign our print ad so that it looks like our competitor's. People will notice it by thinking we're the competition"
(Client, to Creative Director)

"I know our logo fucks up your design, but still put it in there. Big bigger than all other graphics"
(Client to Designer)

"You have 'forum' capitalized here. It should be lower case" - "Yes but it's our forum" - "But it's not the Forum in Rome, it's just a meeting" - "It's our convention to capitalize it, so please do so"

(Client speaking with Creative Director, after "reworking" body copy -per the Chicago style guide- of a print ad)

"You can't really touch the placing of all the information on the screen, everything has been researched and tested already. We want you to decide on the colour of the lines and dividers. They can be dark blue or black or whatever. That's up to you"
(Client's brief to Designer)

"Summarizing: you have to come up with three 30 sec. film scripts with all those benefits that I told you about. But before you do that, please send me few sentences of what you are going to come up with so I can send it to the Client as he has to get used to what you are going to come up with"

(Agency, Account Executive to Creative Director)

> "I'm not sure what the client wants, so let's try and do something the client will buy"
>
> (Agency, Senior Account Executive to Copywriter)

> "The client has given us FINAL approval, but asked if we could change one small thing"
>
> (Agency, Project Manager to Art Director)

"Yeah, We don't like the orange color. Can't we just fade red into the yellow?"
(Client, giving direction to Designer)

"This print ad must be a mix between what is there and what is not there"
(Agency, Account Supervisor)

"You can't say no, you're the agency"

(Client, to Account Supervisor, when he asked that it's OK to ask for what they want 100% of the time and just be ready to be told ´no´)

"I need the background to be transparent. I have some transparencies that you can scan so you can have a transparent layer in Photoshop"

(Agency, Boss offering help to bewildered designer)

"I asked for a printing budget in 2 colors and in 4 colors" - *"And what colors are those going to be?"*

(Agency, conversation between Designer and Chief of Production)

"Well, actually, we have to say this but without saying it"

(Agency, Account Executive, briefing)

"I want you to surprise me with something I've never seen before. I want you to invent the wheel, just visually"
(Agency, Creative director to designer finishing a brochure, first week at her new job. Then he left for a party)

"Can you change the word 'exquisite' on the ad? Words including the letter X are way too complicated"
(Client, Marketing Manager)

"The reflections in the water should be at angle opposite to the sun" - "Um, no. The SHADOWS of objects would be at an angle away from the sun, but a reflection is always perpendicular to the reflective surface" - "No, you're wrong. Go back and point all the reflections away from the sun" - "Well, that would start to look kind of strange. Say, I have a small mirror at my desk; let me go get it so I can show you what I mean…" - "Don't get difficult with me!"

(Conversation with Client, looking at a Photoshop image)

"Add a roll-over state. People love roll-overs" - "Well, if that's the case, why don't we add puppies to the ad? Because everyone loves puppies"

(Agency, Associate Creative Director to Copywriter, asking to add unnecessary fluff to a basic banner)

"We need a giant steam head rising above the booth" - "Why?" - "Because people love steam. They're drawn to it. It's the power and magic of steam I'm talking about here!"

(Client, to Agency President)

"Overall, it's a great ad. But I don't like the headline, and I don't like the layout" - "What do you like? The border?" - "Well… yes"
(Conversation between Client and Agency)

You can visit - *and contribute, if you are up to it!* - the live and updated Tumblr version of **ADverbatims** here, enjoy:

 http://adverbatims.tumblr.com

Icons by
Gregor Cresnar
Anton Håkanson
Razmik Badalyan
Lorie Shaull
Delwar Hossain
Karthik Srinivas
Guilherme Simoes
Gan Khoon Lay
Chameleon Design
Gianni - Dolce Merda
Nick Kinling
Karthik Srinivas
from Noun Project